GUNS N' ROSES
APPETITE FOR DESTRUCTION

Photography by Neil Zlozower

Cherry Lane Music Company
Director of Publications/Project Editor: Mark Phillips

ISBN 978-1-4803-3391-8

Visit our website at www.cherrylaneprint.com

CONTENTS

EDITOR'S NOTE: The songs in this collection are written a half step higher than the key of the recording. Guns N' Roses play the songs in these written keys, but since their instruments are retuned, the recorded music sounds lower.

W. Axl Rose

Slash

Neil Zlozower

Izzy Stradlin'

Neil Zlozower

Duff "Rose" McKagan

Steven Adler

Welcome to the Jungle

Words and Music by
W. Axl Rose, Slash,
Izzy Stradlin', Duff McKagan
and Steven Adler

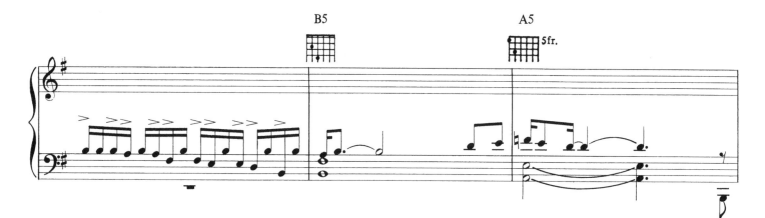

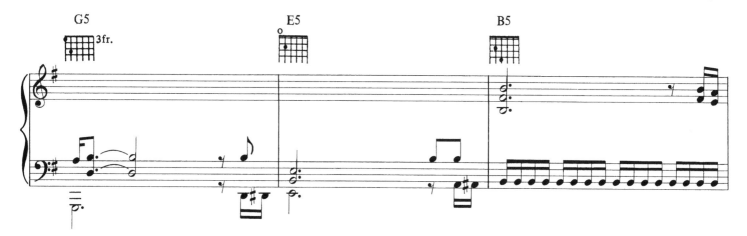

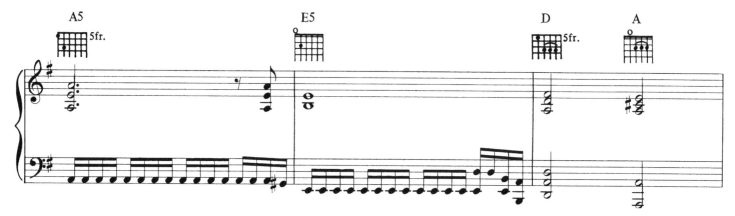

Faster ♩ = 124

1. Wel-come   to the   jun - gle,   we got   fun 'n'   games.____
2.3. *See additional lyrics*

We got   ev - 'ry - thing__ you want,__   hon - ey, we   know the names.__ We   are the

9

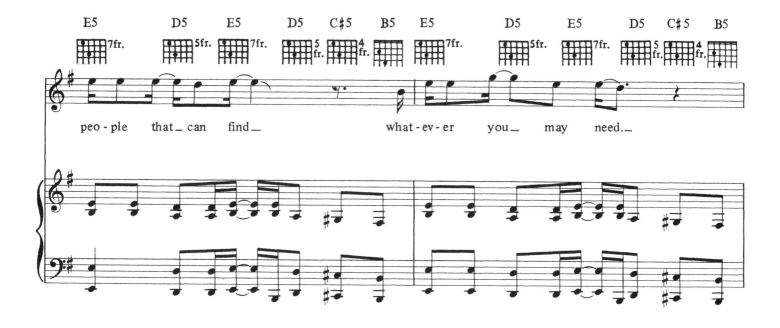

peo - ple that can find whatever you may need.

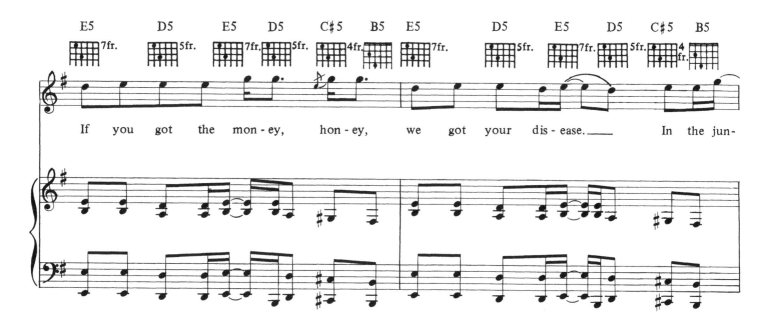

If you got the mon - ey, hon - ey, we got your dis - ease. In the jun-

gle. Wel - come to the jun - gle. Watch it bring you to your

sha na na na na na na na na na na knees,   knees.

Uh,   ah.   I wan-na watch   you__ bleed.

I wan-na hear   you__ scream!

[3.]

D   G

I'm gon-na watch you bleed!

Bridge

D   G   D

And when you're high____

G   D   G   F

____ you nev - er   ev - er want to come down,____   so

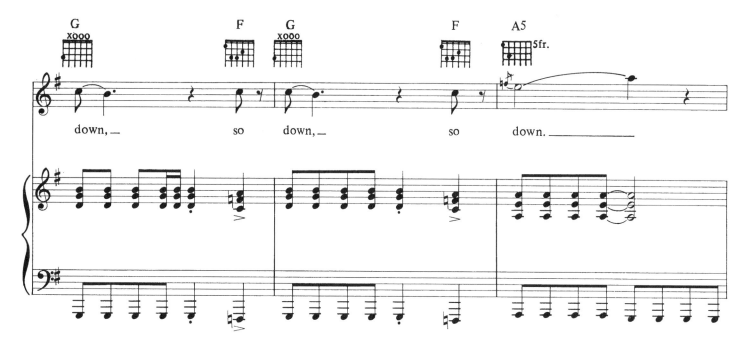

down, _____ so down, _____ so down. _____

Yeah! _____

_____ Now!

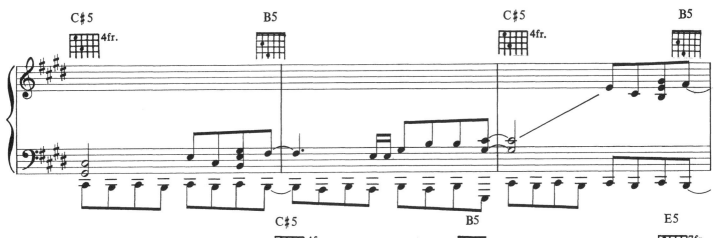
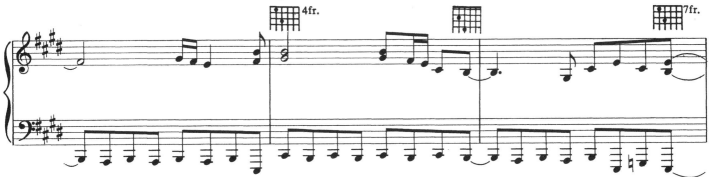

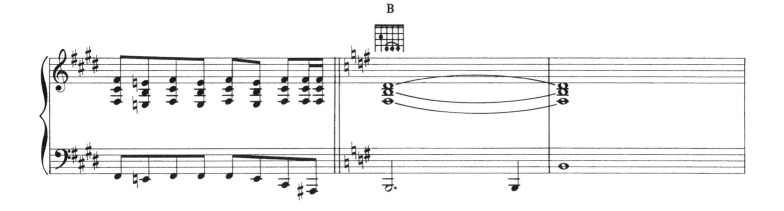

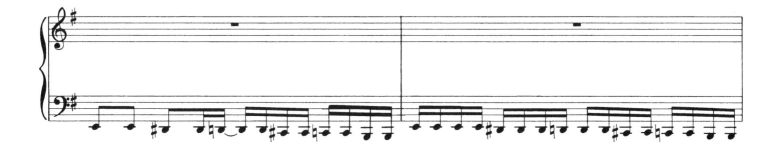

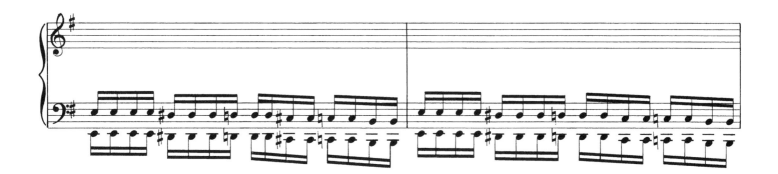

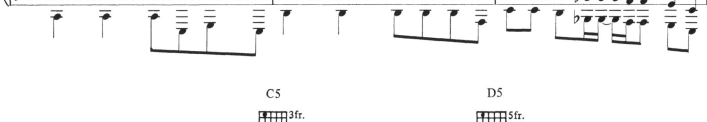

Additional Lyrics

2. Welcome to the jungle, we take it day by day.
   If you want it, you're gonna bleed, but it's the price you pay.
   And you're a very sexy girl who's very hard to please.
   You can taste the bright lights, but you won't get them for free.
   In the jungle. Welcome to the jungle.
   Feel my, my, my serpentine.
   I wanna hear you scream!

3. Welcome to the jungle, it gets worse here every day.
   You learn to live like an animal in the jungle where we play.
   If you got a hunger for what you see, you'll take it eventually,
   You can have anything you want, but you better not take it from me.
   In the jungle. Welcome to the jungle.
   Watch it bring you to your sha na na na na na na na na na na na knees, knees.
   I'm gonna watch you bleed! *(To Bridge)*

It's So Easy

Words and Music by
W. Axl Rose, Slash,
Izzy Stradlin', Duff McKagan,
Steven Adler and West Arkeen

Moderately fast ♩ = 152

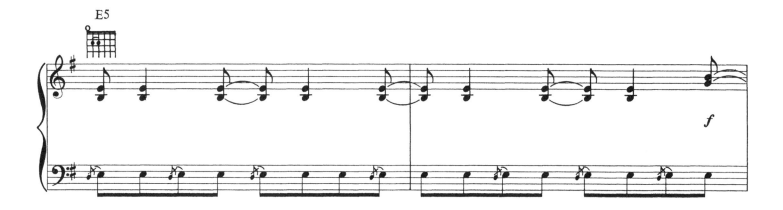

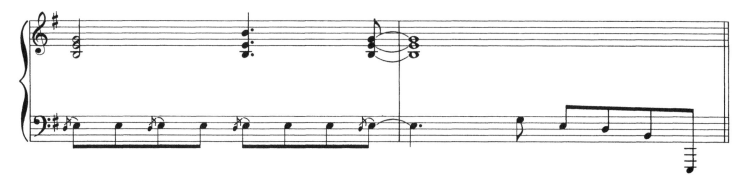

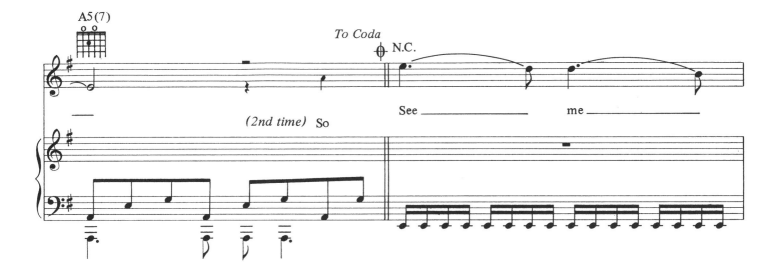

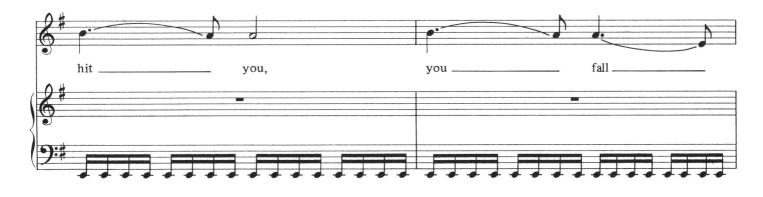

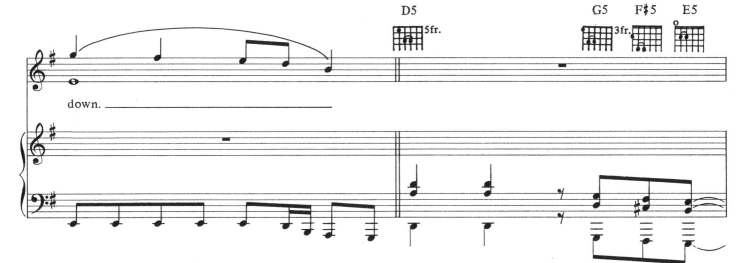

You think you're___ so cool.

Why don't you___ just

fuck off?___

(Lead gtr. ad lib)

24

no mon-ey but it goes__ to show.__

It's so__ eas - y.   So fuck-in' eas - y.

It's so__ eas - y.

So damn__ eas - y.   It's so__ eas - y.

So fuck - in' eas - y.

It's so_____ eas - y.

Yeah!__

Additional Lyrics

2. Cars are crashin' every night.
   I drink 'n' drive, everything's in sight.
   I make the fire, but I miss the firefight.
   I hit the bull's-eye every night. *(To Chorus)*

3. Ya get nothin' for nothin', if that's what ya do.
   Turn around bitch, I got a use for you.
   Besides, you ain't got nothin' better to do,
   And I'm bored. *(To Chorus)*

Nightrain

Words and Music by
W. Axl Rose, Slash,
Izzy Stradlin', Duff McKagan
and Steven Adler

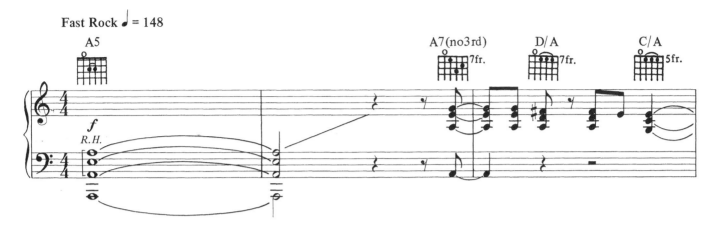

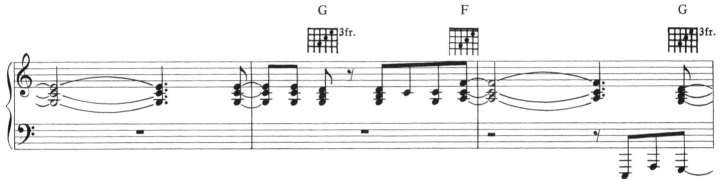

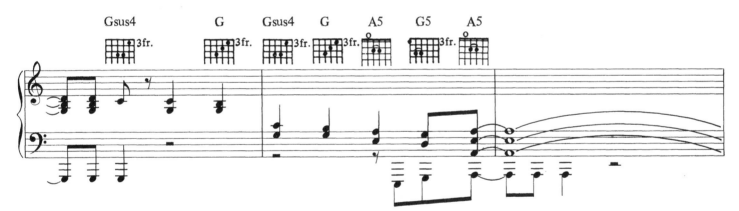

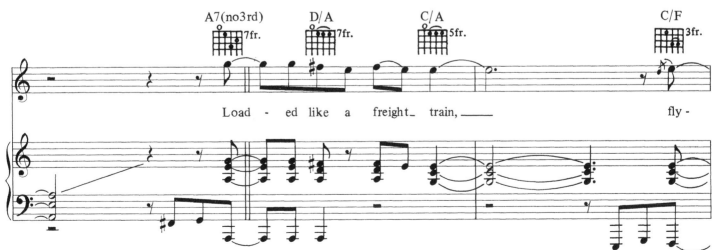

Load - ed like a freight_ train,_____ fly -

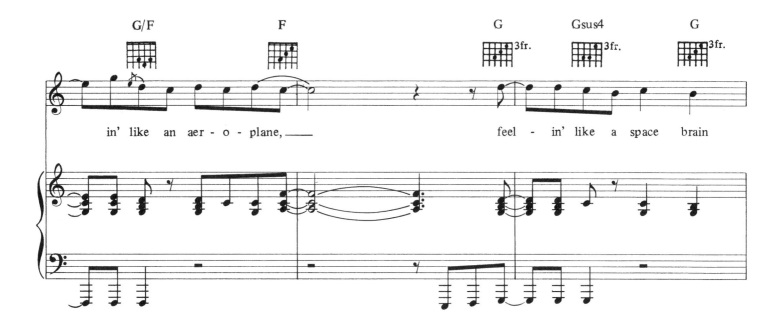

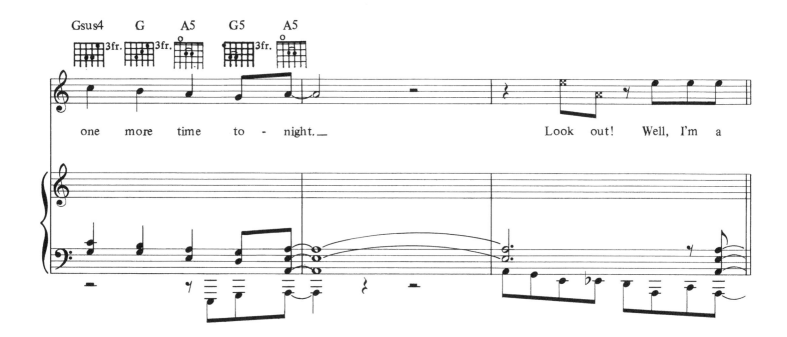

un-der my arm.___ Said I'm a mean ma - chine,___ been drink-in' gas - o - line,___ an' hon-ey,

you can make my mo - tor hum.___ Well, I got one chance left___ in a
Wake up late,___ hon - ey,

nine live cat.___ I got a, a dog - eat - dog sly smile.___ I got a
put on your clothes___ and take your cred - it card___ to the liq - uor store.___ Well, that's

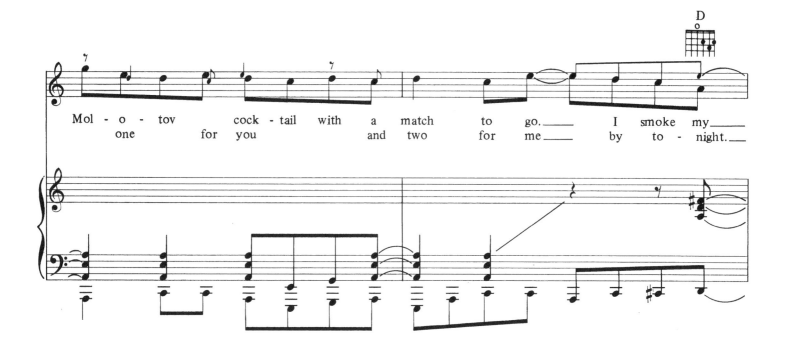

Mol - o - tov cock - tail with a match to go.___ I smoke my___
one for you and two for me___ by to - night.___

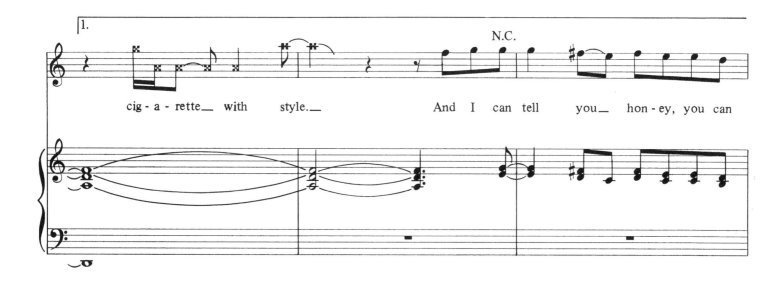

cig - a - rette___ with style.___ And I can tell you___ hon - ey, you can

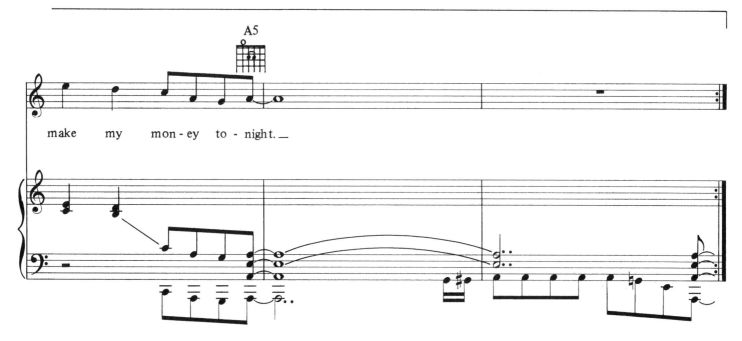

make my mon - ey to - night.___

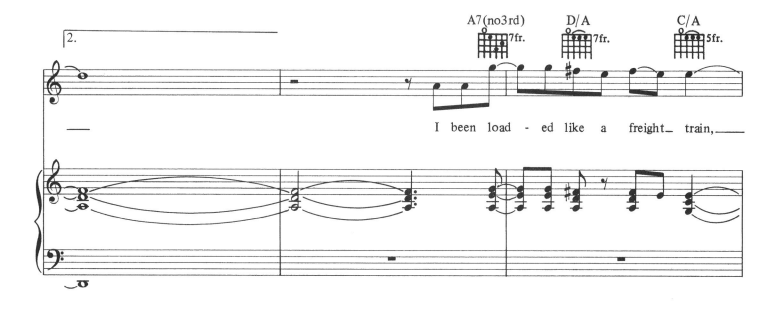

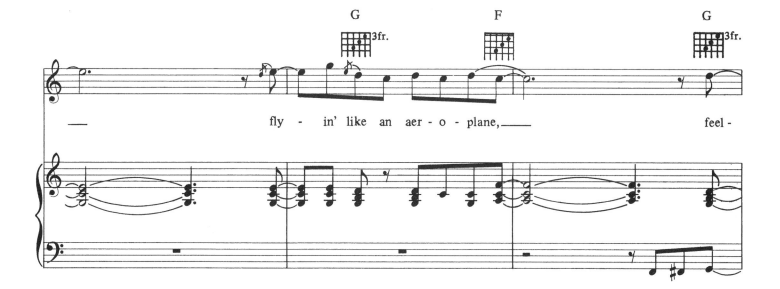

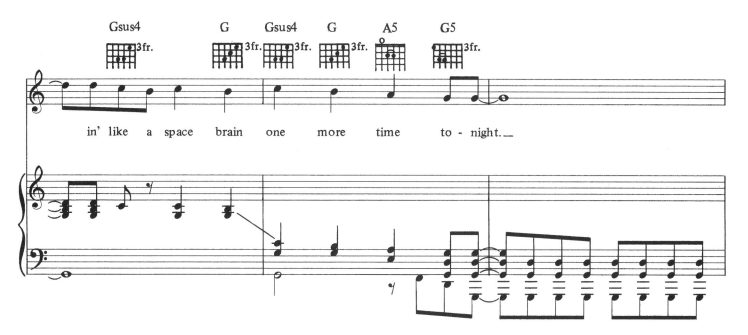

I'm on the night-train.   Bot-toms   up.__ I'm on the
night-train.   I love that   stuff.__ I'm on the

night-train.   Fill   my   cup.__ I'm on the night-train,
night-train____ and I can nev - er get e - nough.__ I'm on the night-train,

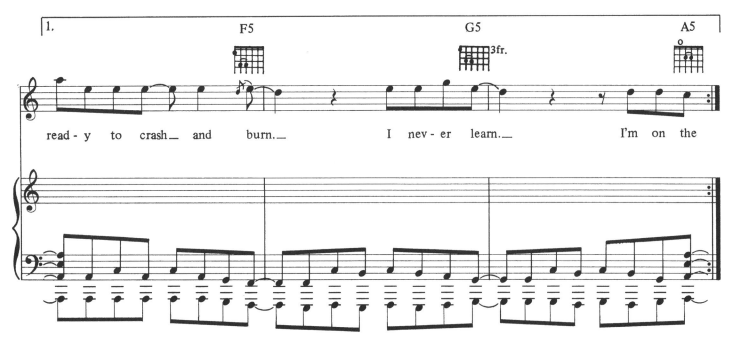

read - y to crash__ and burn.__   I nev - er learn.__   I'm on the

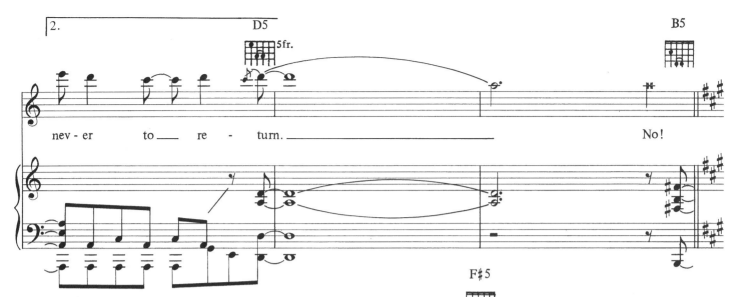

never to re - turn. _____ No!

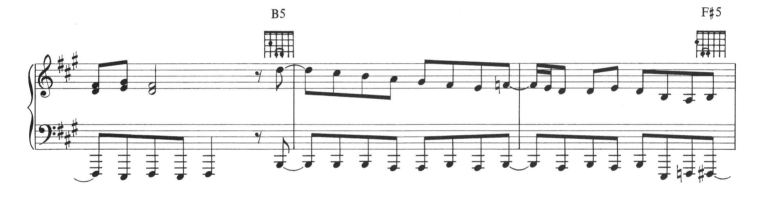

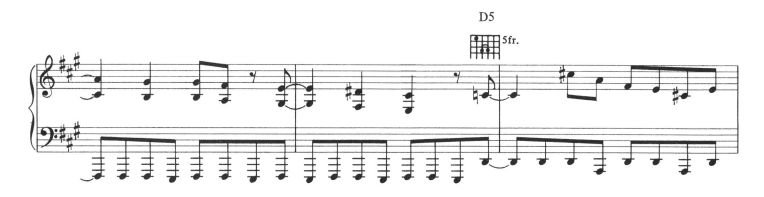

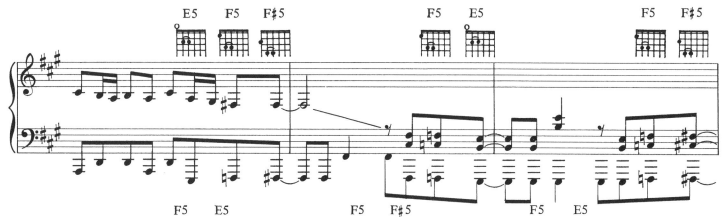

Load - ed like a freight_ train,_

fly - in' like an aer - o - plane,_____ speed-

in' like a space brain one more time to - night._____

Additional Lyrics

Nightrain, bottom's up.
I'm on the nightrain, fill my cup.
I'm on the nightrain, whoa yeah!

I'm on the nightrain, love that stuff.
I'm on the nightrain, and I can never get enough.
Ridin' the nightrain, I guess I,
I guess, I guess, I guess I never learn.

On the nightrain, float me home.
Oh, I'm on the nightrain.
Ridin' the nightrain, never to return.

Nightrain.

Out ta Get Me

Words and Music by
W. Axl Rose, Slash,
Izzy Stradlin', Duff McKagan
and Steven Adler

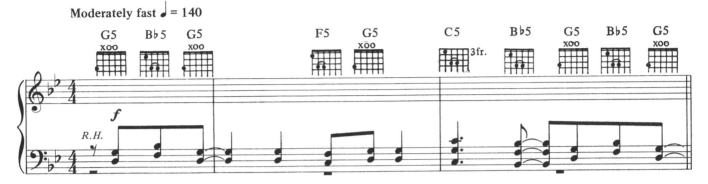

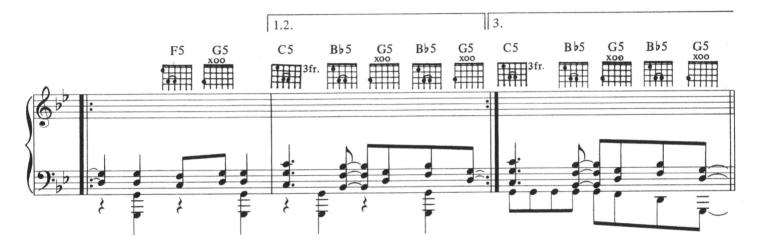

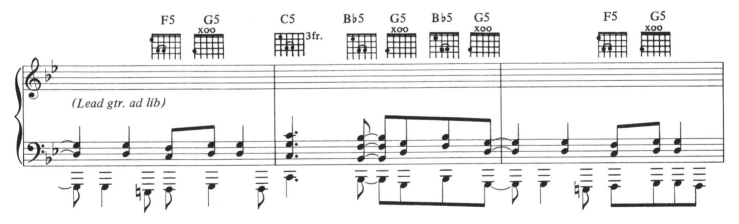

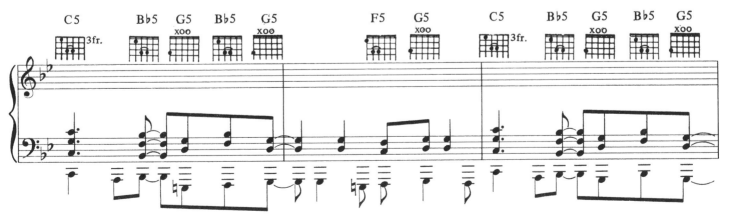

Been hid-in' out_ and_
Some-times it's eas-y to for -

lay-in' low._ It's noth-in' new_ to me.___
get where you're go-in', some-times it's hard-er to leave.___

(end gtr. solo)

Well, you can al - ways find a place to go, __
And ev - 'ry time you think you know just what you're do - in',

if you can keep your san-i-ty.___ They break down the doors___ and they
that's when your trou-bles ex-ceed.___ They push me in a cor-ner just to

rape my rights___ but (they__won't touch me).___ Just scream and yell___ and
get me to fight___ but (they__won't touch me.)___ They preach and yell___ and

fight all night. ___
fight all night. ___ }
(You ___ can't tell me.)___

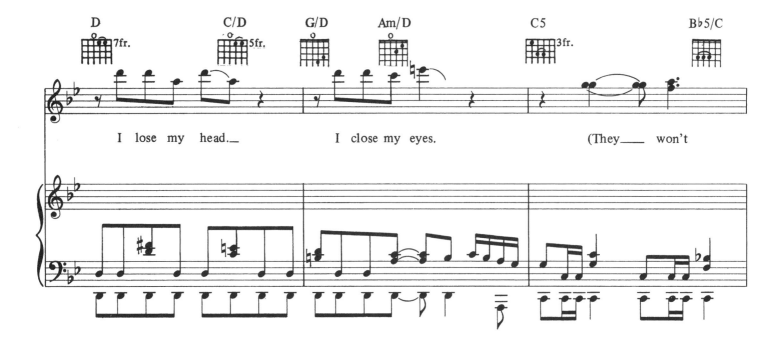

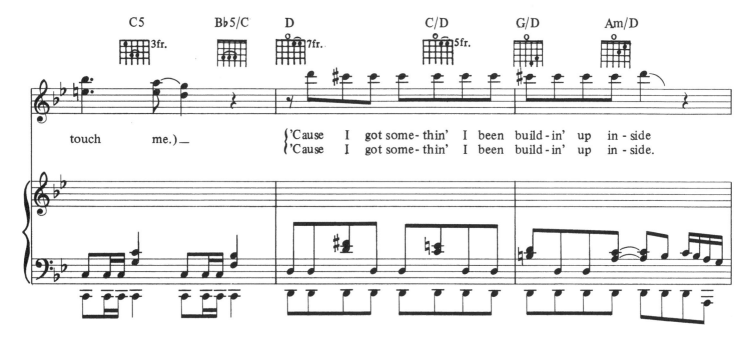

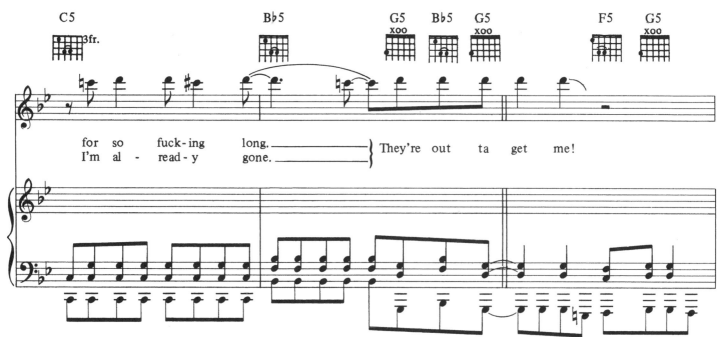

They won't catch me! I'm fuck - in'

in - no - cent!___ They won't break___ me!

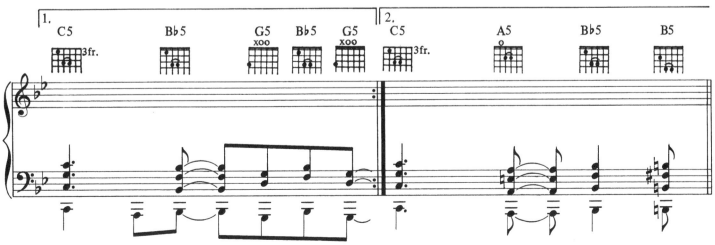

Lem - me   see   ya   try.

Some peo-ple got a chip on their shoul-der

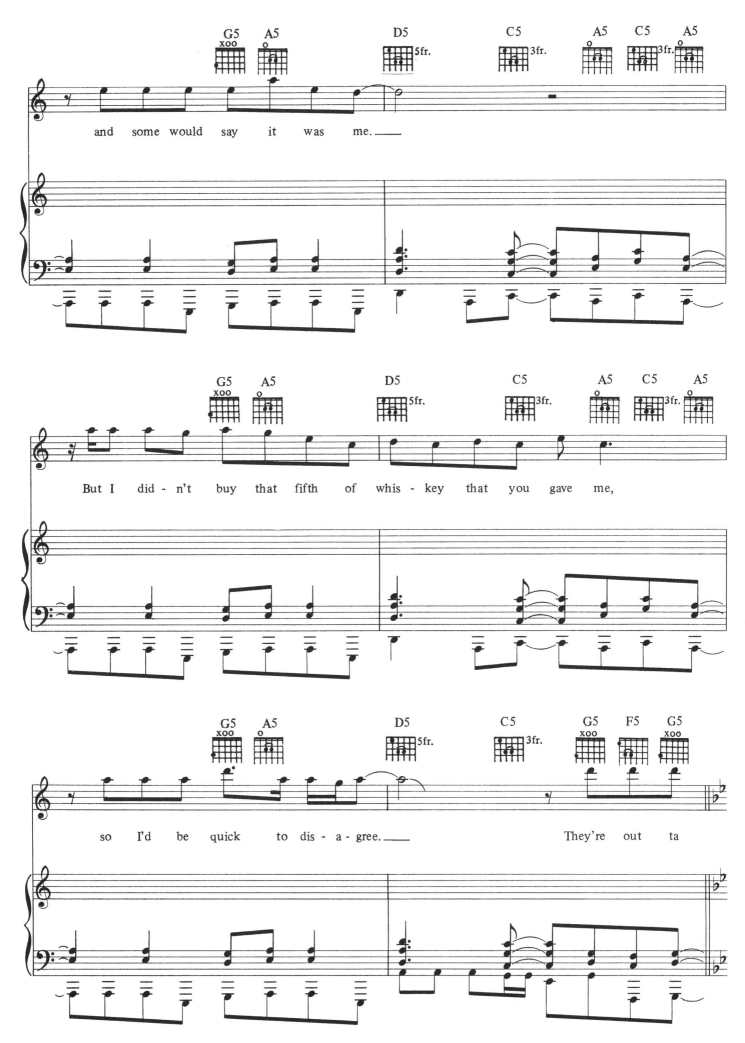

and some would say it was me. ___

But I did - n't buy that fifth of whis - key that you gave me,

so I'd be quick to dis - a - gree. ___ They're out ta

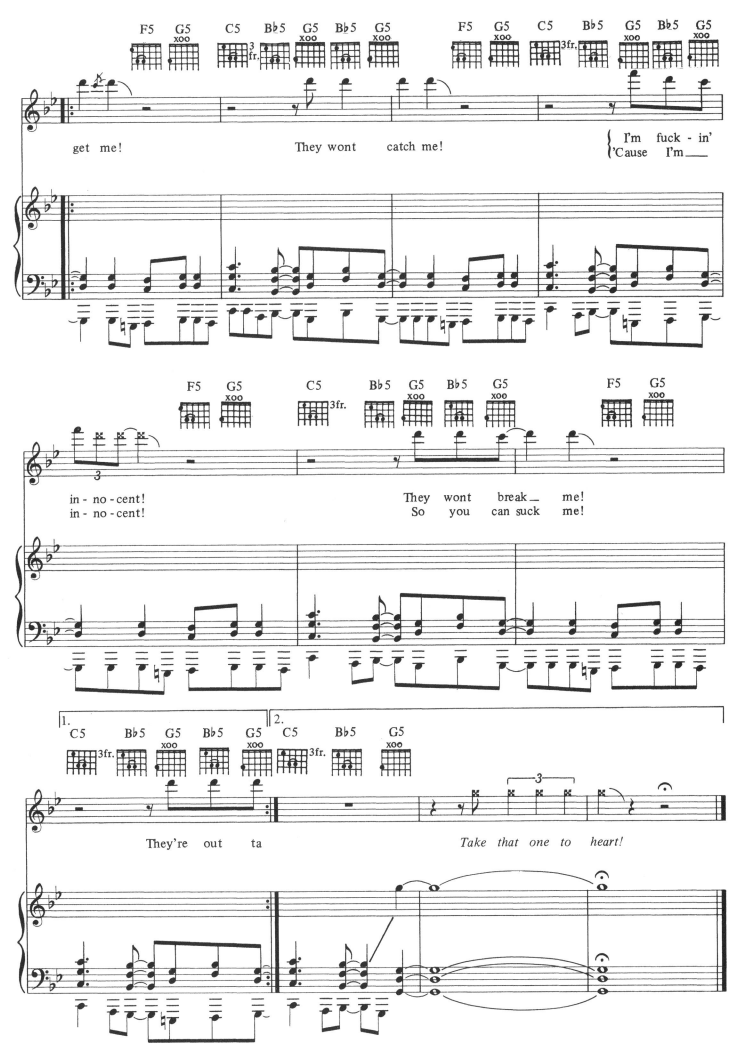

Mr. Brownstone

Words and Music by
W. Axl Rose, Slash,
Izzy Stradlin', Duff McKagan
and Steven Adler

I get up _ a-round sev-en,   get out-ta bed_ a-round nine.   And
u-su'lly starts_ a-round sev-en.   We go on stage_ a-round nine.

I don't wor-ry a-bout noth-in', no,_ be-cause wor-ry-in's a waste_ of my   time.
Get on the bus a-round e-lev-en sip-pin' a drink_ and feel - in'   fine.

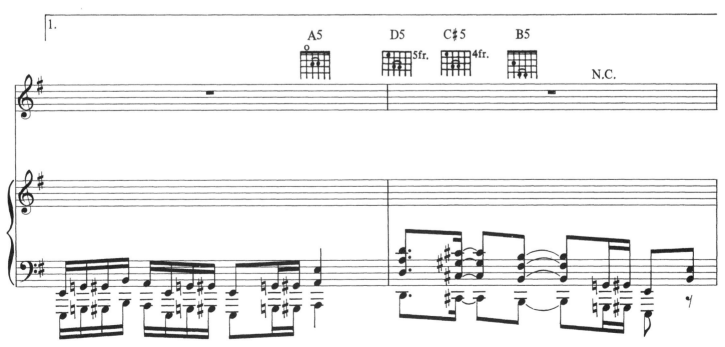

1.

A5   D5   C#5   B5

N.C.

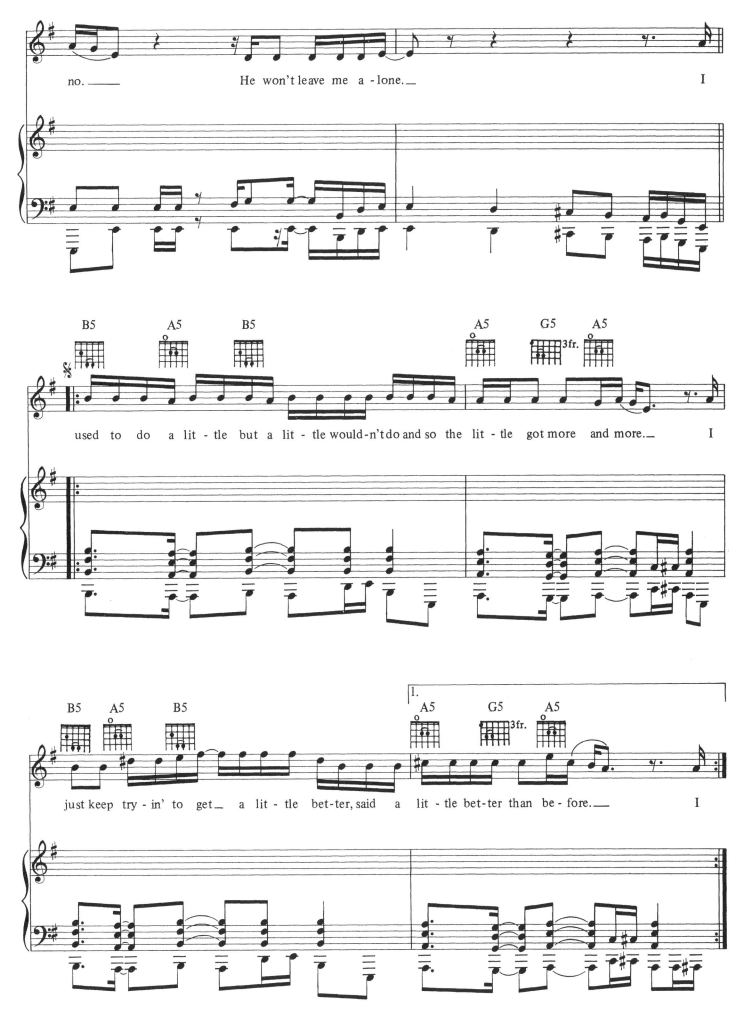

no. _____ He won't leave me a - lone. _____ I

used to do a lit - tle but a lit - tle would-n't do and so the lit - tle got more and more. _____ I

just keep try - in' to get _ a lit - tle bet - ter, said a lit - tle bet - ter than be - fore. _____ I

51

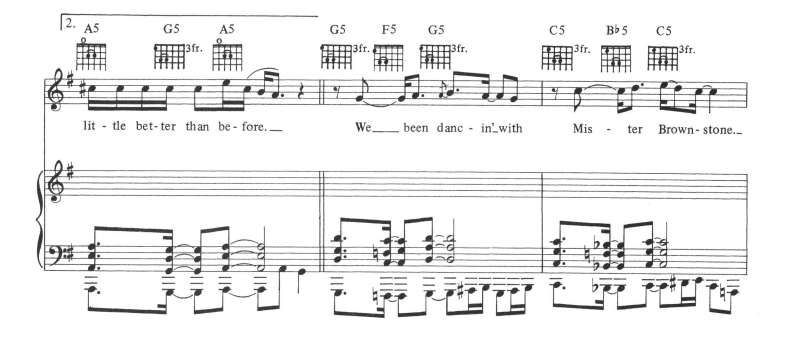

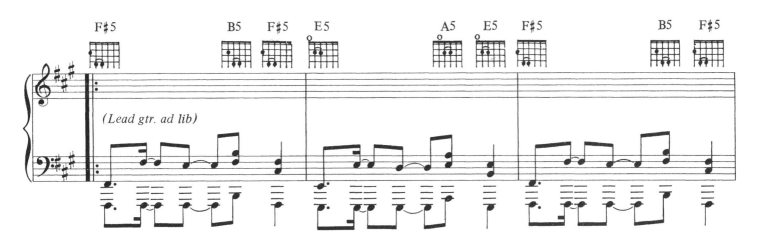

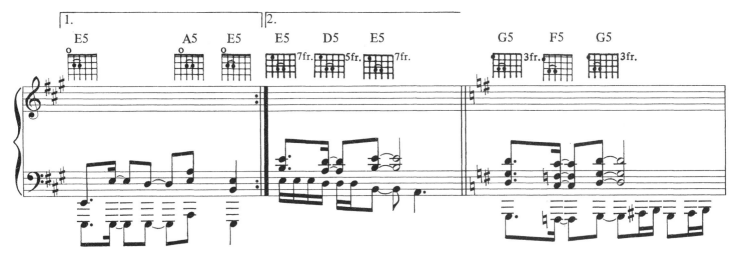

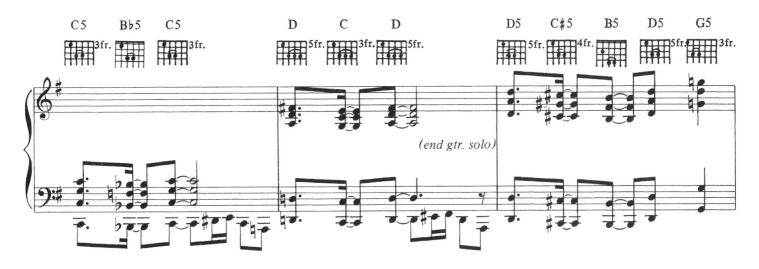

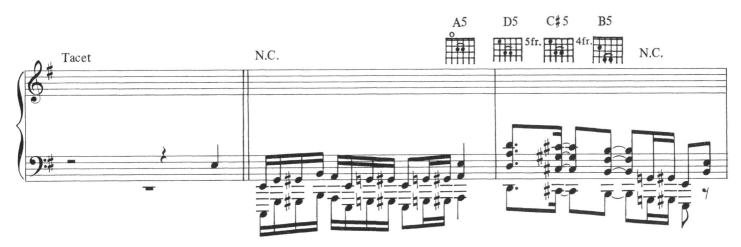

53

Now I get up_ a - round when-ev - er. I used to get up_ on time. But

that old man,_ he's a real muth - a - fuck - er gon - na kick him on down the line.____ I

Paradise City

Words and Music by
W. Axl Rose, Slash,
Izzy Stradlin', Duff McKagan
and Steven Adler

Take me down_ to the par - a - dise ci - ty, where the grass is green and the girls are pret - ty.

Oh, won't you please take me home. _____

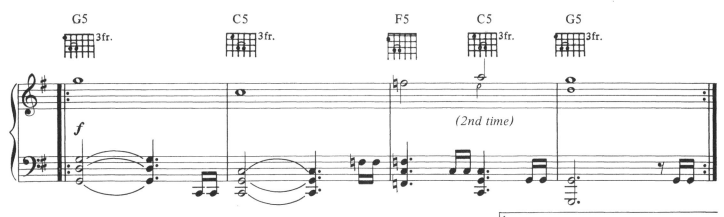

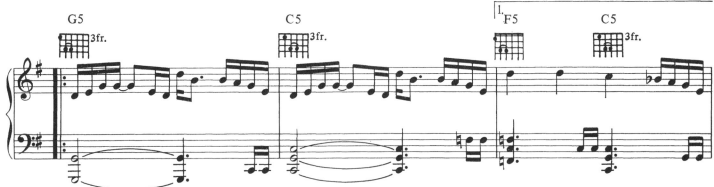

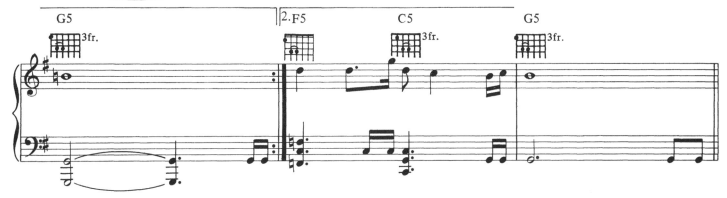

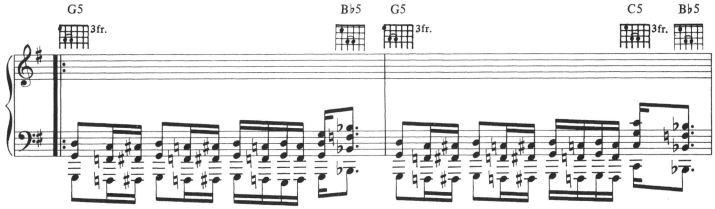

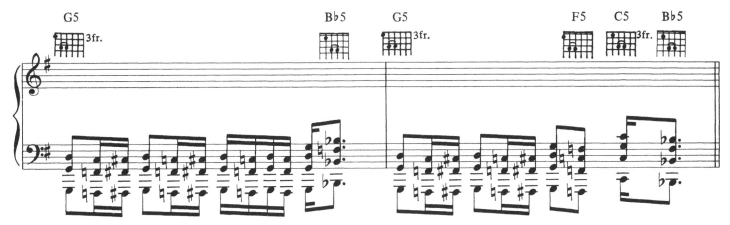

1. Just a ur-chin liv-in' un-der the street. I'm a ____ hard case thats tough to beat. ____ I'm your
2.3.4. *See additional lyrics*

char - i - ty case, ____ so buy me some-thing to eat. ____ I'll pay you at an-oth-er time.

1.
Take it to the end of the line. ____

2.
Ev-'ry-bod-y's do-in' their time. ____

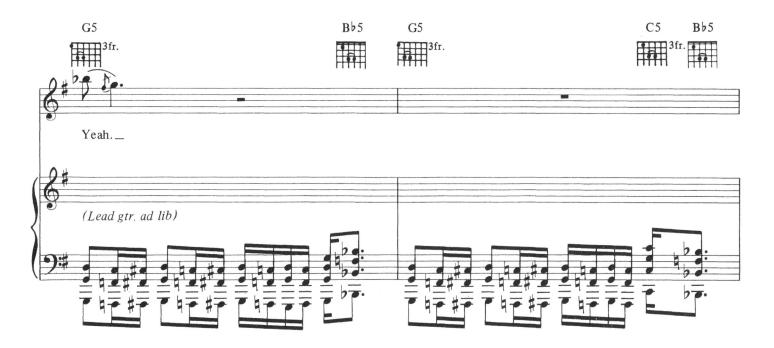

Yeah. —

(Lead gtr. ad lib)

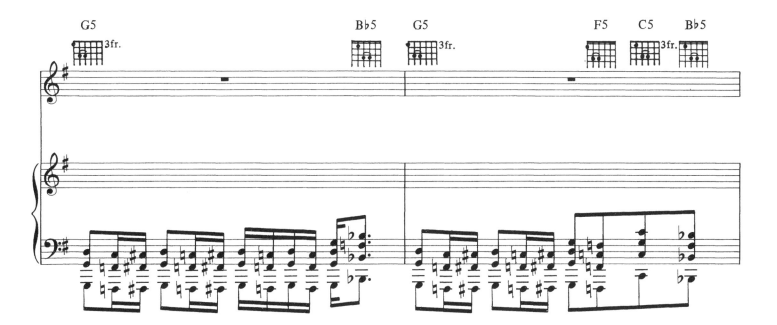

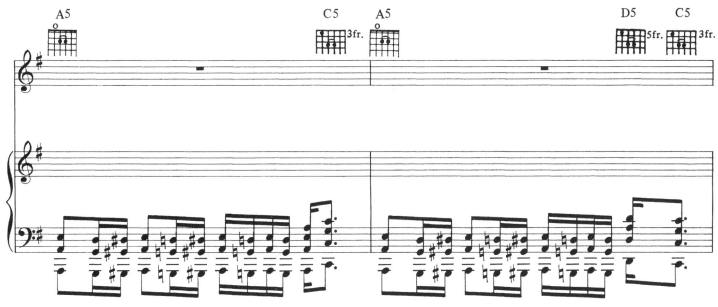

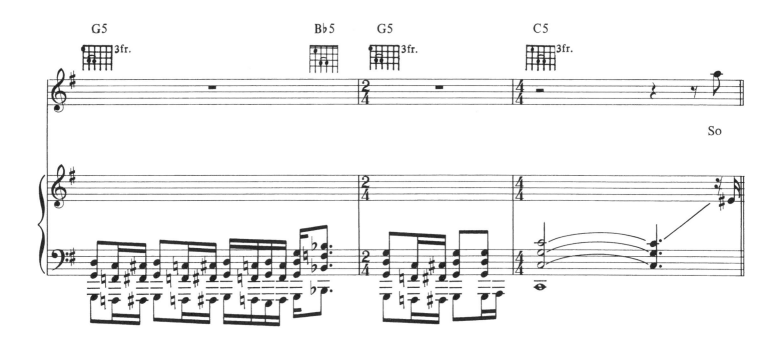

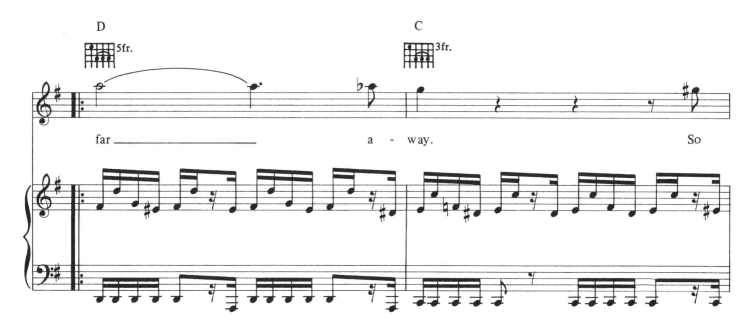

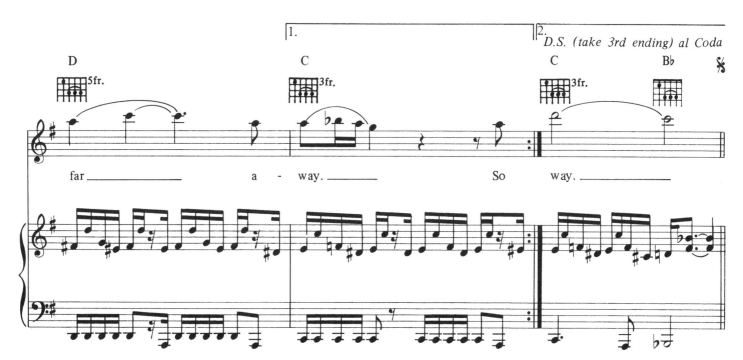

Coda

G5 3fr.

home._____

G5 3fr.

Take me home__ to the par-a-dise cit-y, where the

C5 3fr.

grass is green and the girls are pret-ty.

1. F5   C5 3fr.   G5 3fr.

Take   me   home,_____ yeah,_yeah._

2. F5   C5 3fr.   G5 3fr.

Oh, wont you please   take me   home,_____

home._____

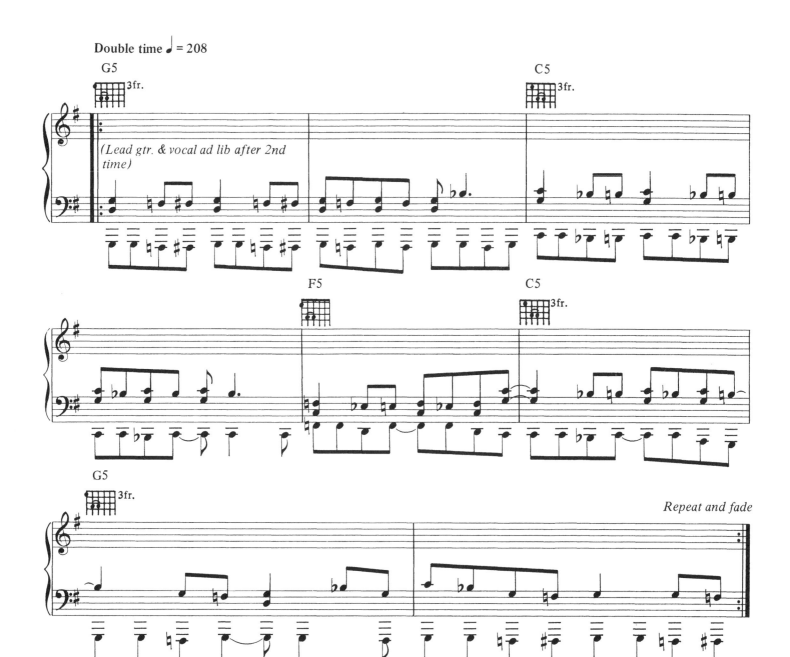

Additional Lyrics

2. Ragz to richez, or so they say.
Ya gotta keep pushin' for the fortune and fame.
It's all a gamble when it's just a game.
Ya treat it like a capital crime.
Everybody's doin' their time. *(To Chorus)*

3. Strapped in the chair of the city's gas chamber,
Why I'm here I can't quite remember.
The surgeon general says it's hazarous to breathe.
I'd have anothe cigarette but I can't see.
Tell me who ya gonna believe? *(To Chorus)*

4. Captain America's been torn a part.
Now he's a court jester with a broken heart.
He said, "Turn me around and take me back to the start."
I must be losin' my mind. "Are you blind?"
I've seen it all a million times. *(To Chorus)*

My Michelle

Words and Music by
W. Axl Rose, Slash,
Izzy Stradlin', Duff McKagan
and Steven Adler

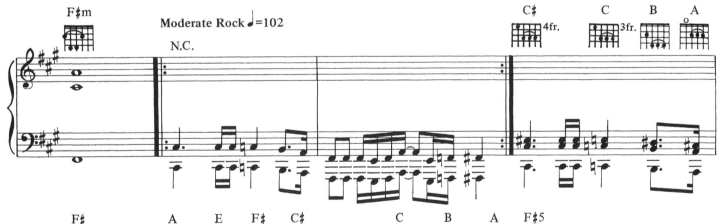

1. Your

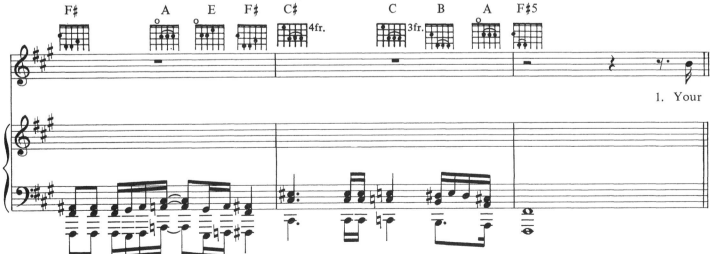

dad - dy works_ in por - no now that mom-my's not_ a round. She

2.3. *See additional lyrics*

used to love_ her her - o - in _ but now she's un - der - ground._ So you

stay out late at night,_ and you do your coke for free._

Driv - in' your_ friends cra - zy with your life's in - san - i - ty._

Well, well, well,__ you just can't tell.__

Well, well, well, my Mi - chelle.__ Look out!

Well, well, well,__ you

never can tell. ___ Well, well, well, my Mi - chelle. ___

Ev - 'ry - one needs love. ___

You know that it's true. ___ Some - day you'll find ___ some - one ___ that - 'll

fall in love with you. ___ But, oh the time it takes ___

when you're all a - lone._____ Some - day you'll find___

___ some - one___ that you can call your own. But till then___ ya bet - ter...

D.S. (take 2nd ending) al Coda %
Play 4 times

(Guitar solo ad lib)

69

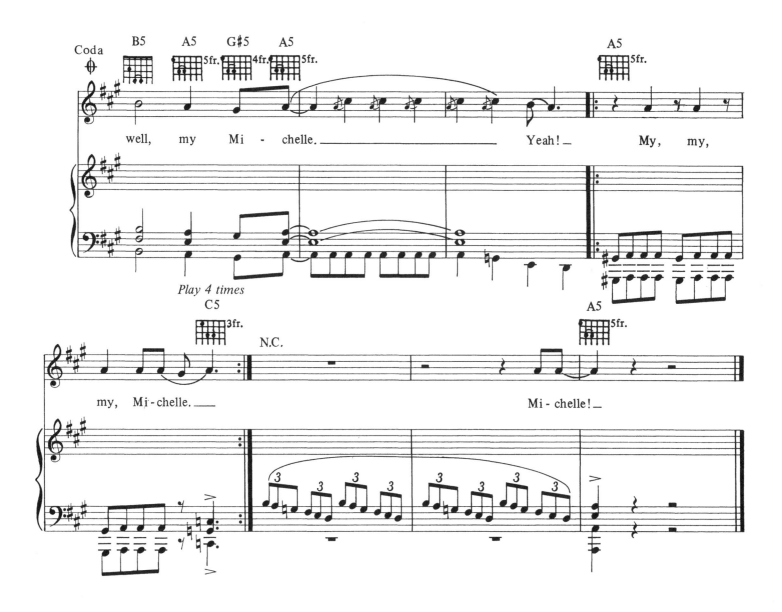

Additional Lyrics

2. Sowin' all your wild oats in another's luxuries.
   Yesterday was Tusday, maybe Thursday you can sleep.
   But school starts much too early, and this hotel wasn't free.
   So party till your connection calls; honey, I'll return the key. *(To Chorus)*

3. Now you're clean and so descreet. I won't say a word.
   But most of all this song is true, case you haven't heard.
   So come on and stop your cryin', 'cause we both know money burns.
   Honey, don't stop tryin' and you'll get what you deserve. *(To Chorus)*

Think About You

Words and Music by
W. Axl Rose, Slash,
Izzy Stradlin', Duff McKagan
and Steven Adler

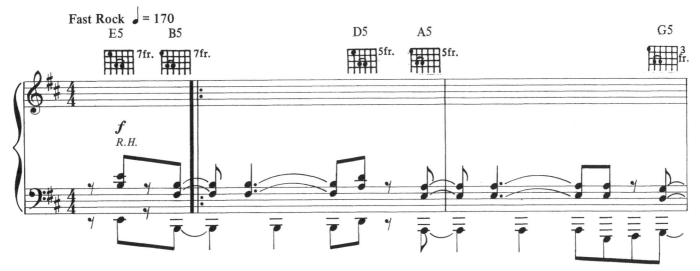

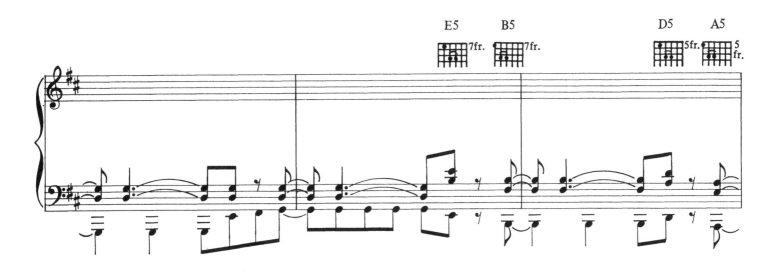

1. I say ba - by, you been look - in' real good,__ you know that I re - mem - ber when we met.__
2.3. *See additional lyrics.*

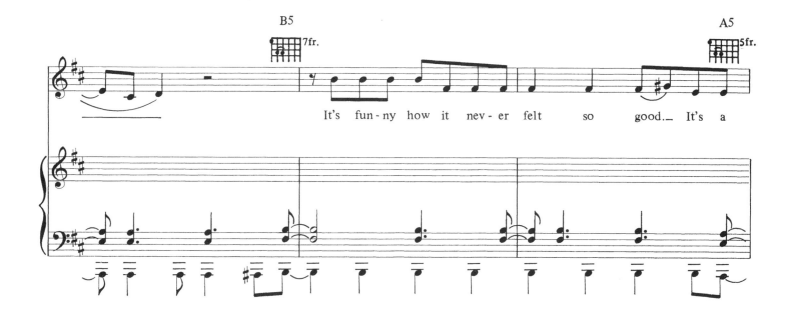

It's fun - ny how it nev - er felt so good.__ It's a

feel - in' that I know, I know I'll nev - er for - get.__ Ooh,_____ it was the

all the time__ my heart__ says yes.__ I think a-bout

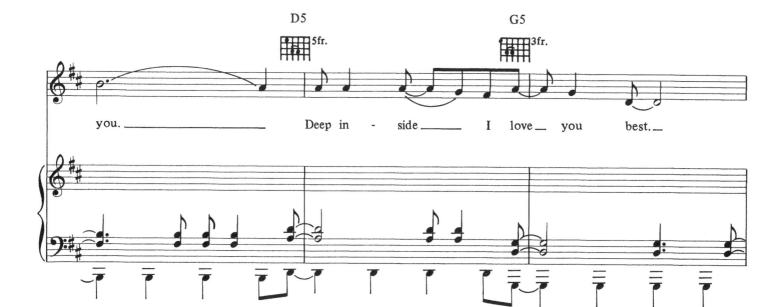

you._____ Deep in - side_____ I love__ you best.__

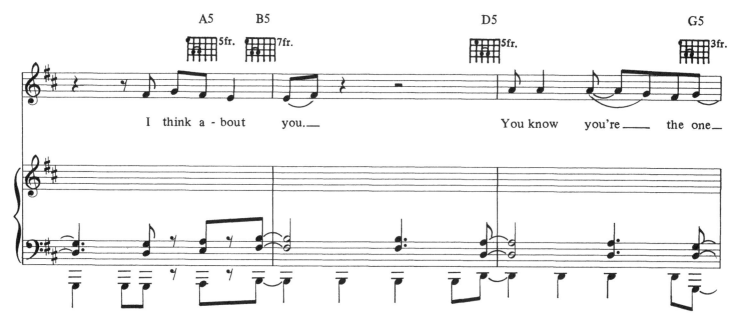

I think a-bout you.__ You know you're____ the one__

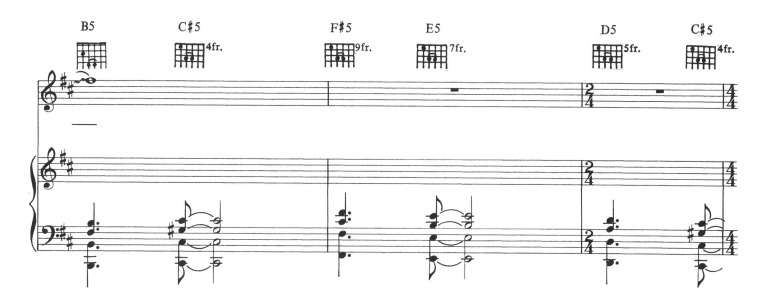

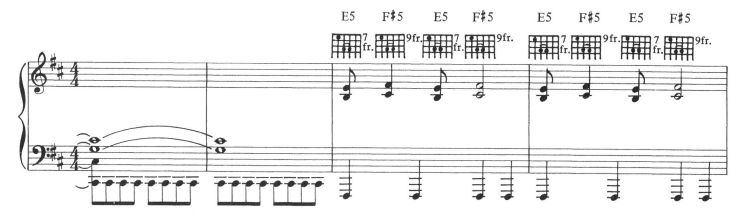

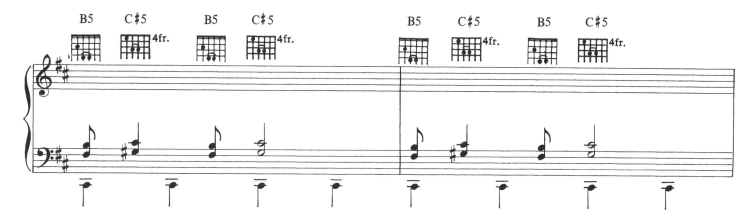

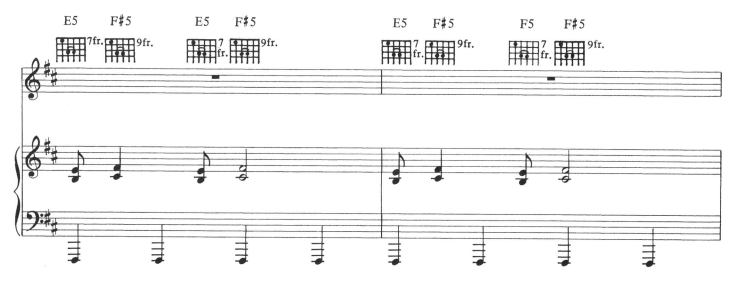

76

it's true.   I think a - bout

D.S. (take 2nd ending) al Coda

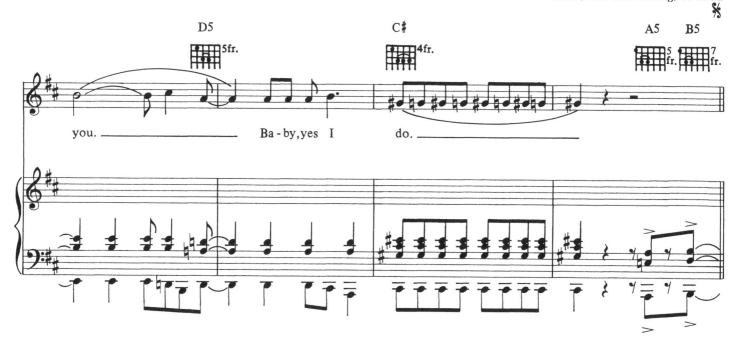

you.   Ba - by, yes I   do.

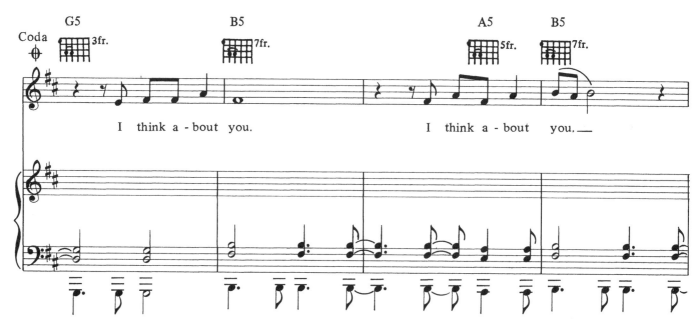

I think a - bout you.   I think a - bout you. ___

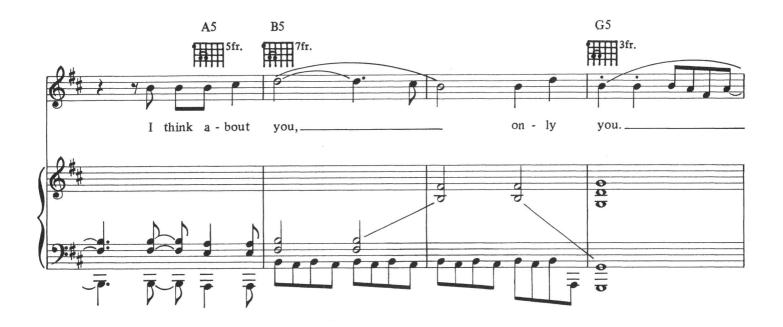

I think a-bout you, ___ on-ly you. ___

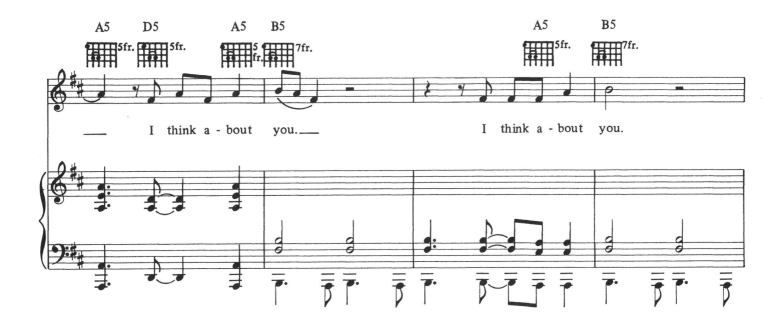

___ I think a-bout you. ___ I think a-bout you.

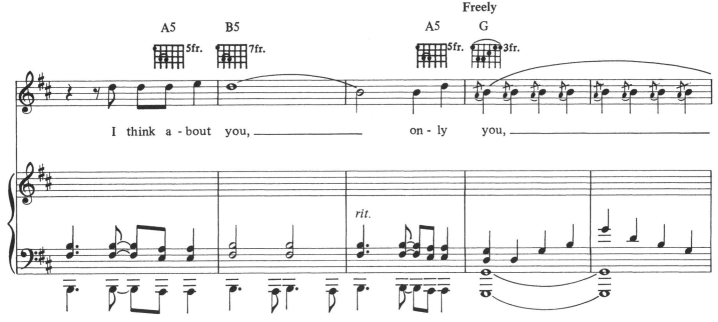

I think a-bout you, ___ on-ly you, ___

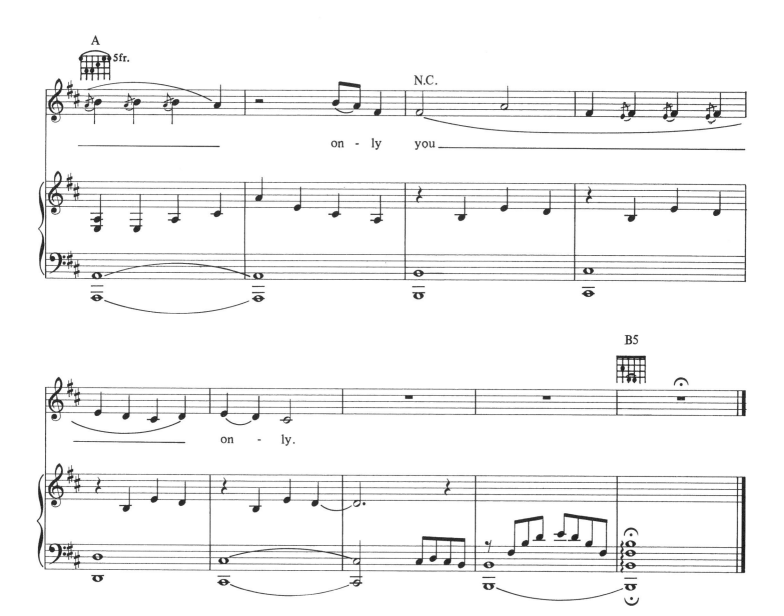

Additional Lyrics

2. There wasn't much in this heart of mine.
   There was a little left and babe, you found it.
   It's funny how I never felt so high,
   It's a feelin' that I know, I know I'll never forget.
   Ooh, it was the best time I can remember, *(etc.)*

3. Somethin' changed in this heart of mine,
   You know that I'm so glad that you showed me.
   Honey, now you're my best friend.
   I want to stay together till the very end.
   Ooh, it was the best time I can remember, *(etc.)*

Sweet Child o' Mine

Words and Music by
W. Axl Rose, Slash,
Izzy Stradlin', Duff McKagan
and Steven Adler

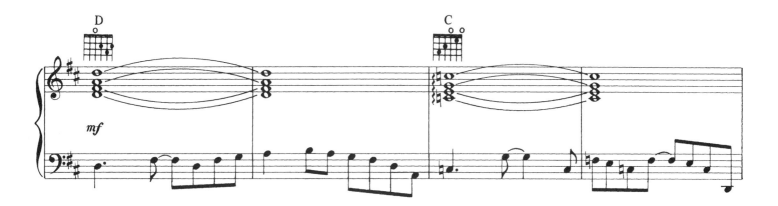

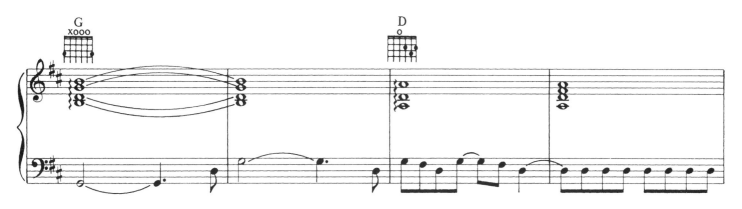

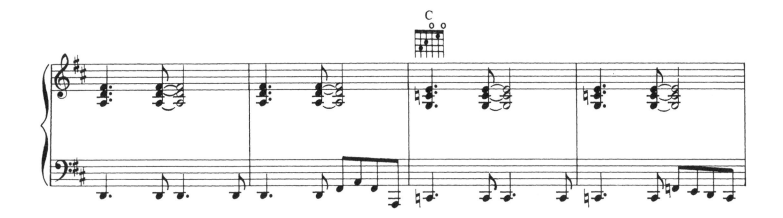

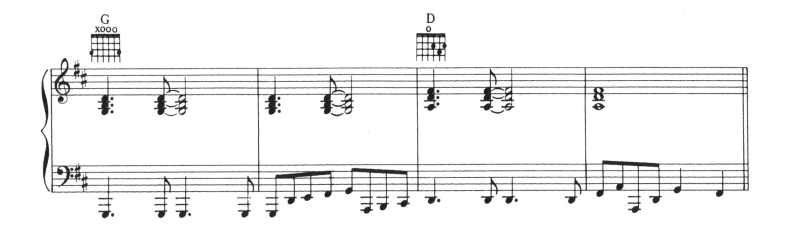

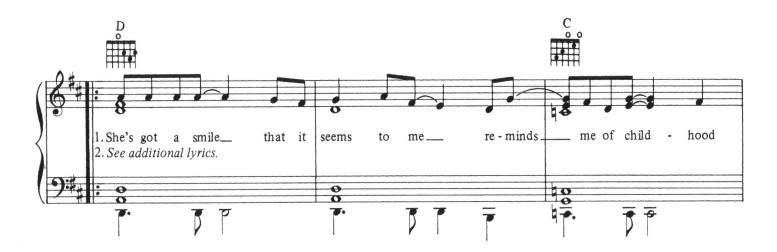

1. She's got a smile__ that it seems to me__ re-minds__ me of child - hood
2. *See additional lyrics.*

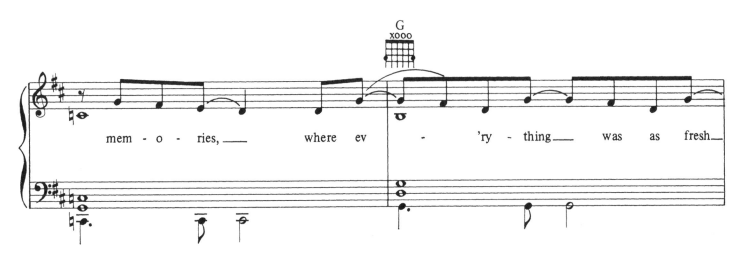

mem - o - ries,__ where ev - 'ry-thing__ was as fresh__

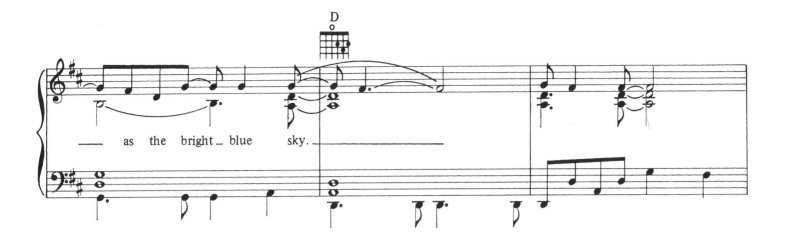

as the bright blue sky.

Now and then __ when I see her face __ she takes me a-way __ to that

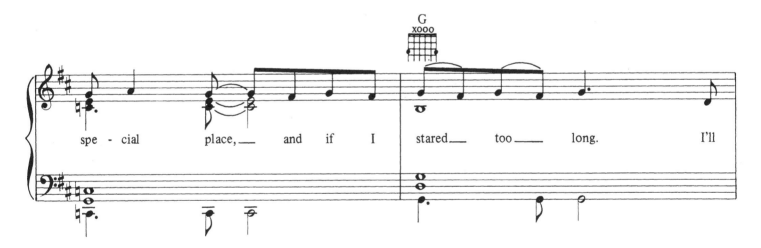

spe - cial place, __ and if I stared __ too __ long. I'll

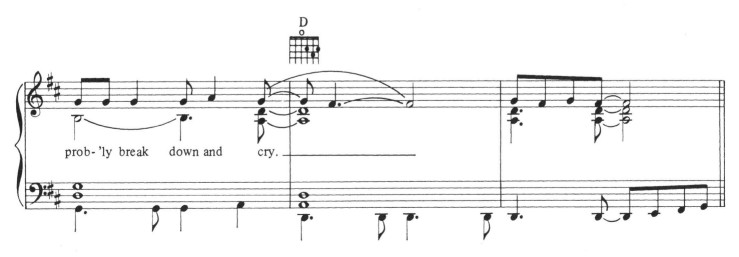

prob-'ly break down and cry. __

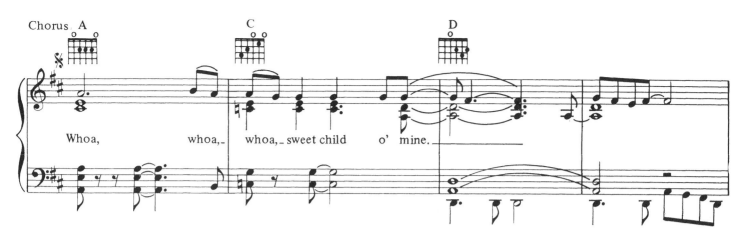

Whoa, whoa, whoa, sweet child o' mine.

Whoa, oh, oh, oh, sweet love o' mine.

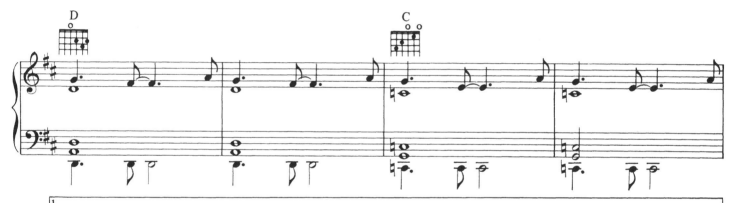

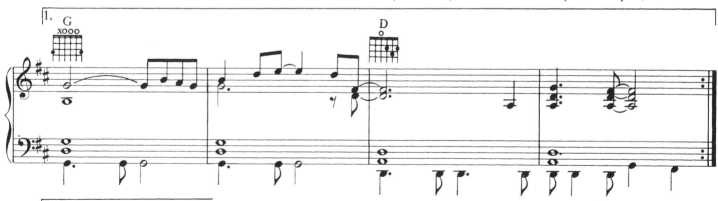

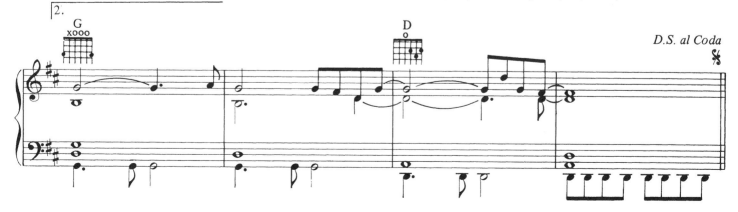

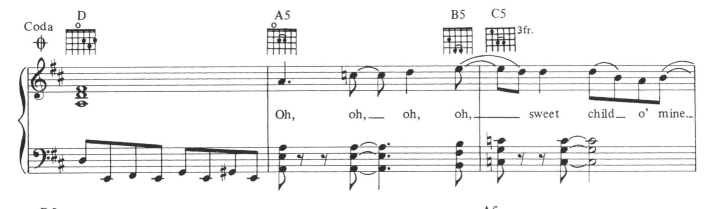

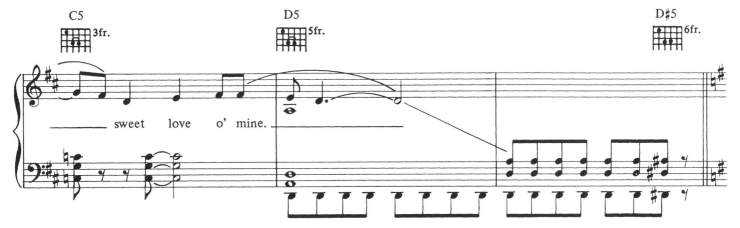

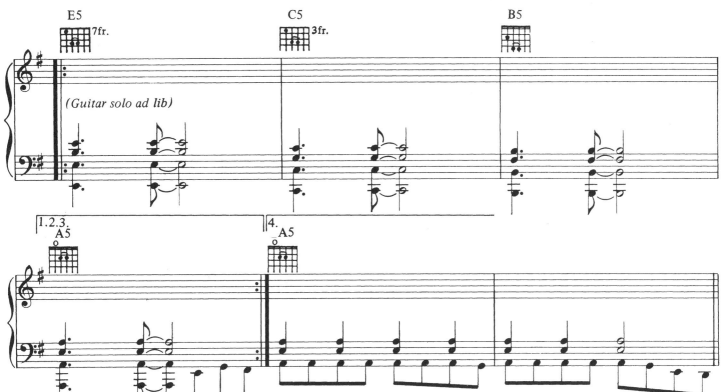

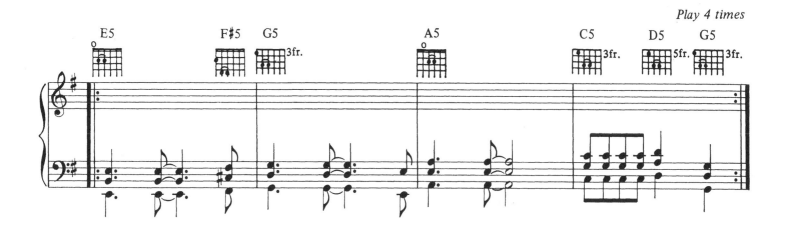

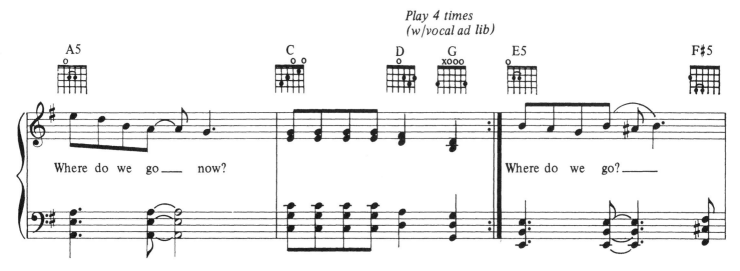

Ah._____ Where do we go___ now? No, no, no, no, no, no,

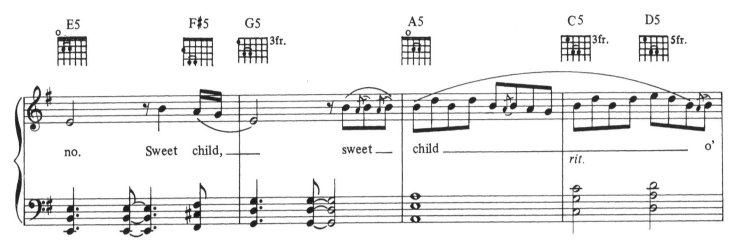

no. Sweet child,_____ sweet __ child _____ o'

rit.

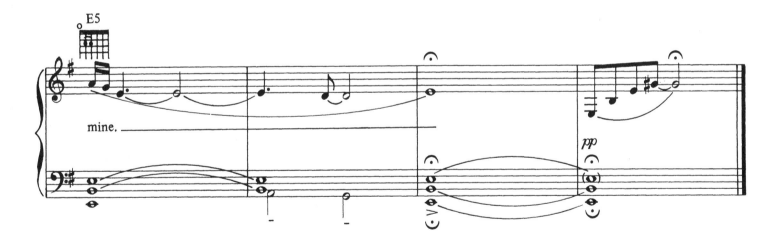

mine. _____

pp

Additional Lyrics

2. She's got eyes of the bluest skies, as if they thought of rain.
   I hate to look into those eyes and see an ounce of pain.
   Her hair reminds me of a warm safe place where as a child I'd hide,
   And pray for the thunder and the rain to quietly pass me by. *(To Chorus)*

You're Crazy

Words and Music by
W. Axl Rose, Slash,
Izzy Stradlin', Duff McKagan
and Steven Adler

88

that's much too dark. ___ You don't ___ want my

love, ___ you want sat - is - fac - tion. Ooh ___

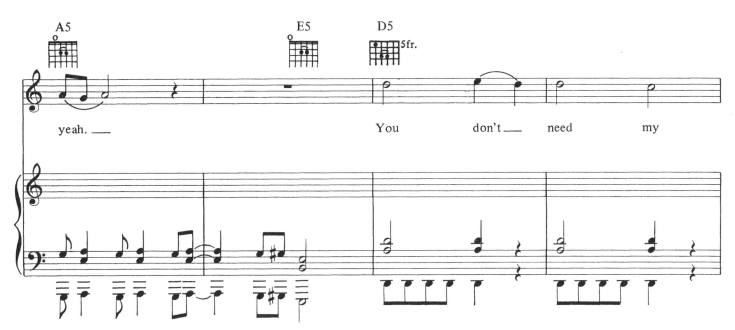

yeah. ___ You don't ___ need my

love, ____ you got - ta find your - self an - oth - er

piece of the ac - tion. ___ Yeah. ___

Half time (♩ = 121)

find your - self an - oth - er

piece of the ac - tion, 'cause you're cra - zy!

You're fuck - in' cra - zy!   Ya know_ you're

cra - zy!   I said you're cra - zy!

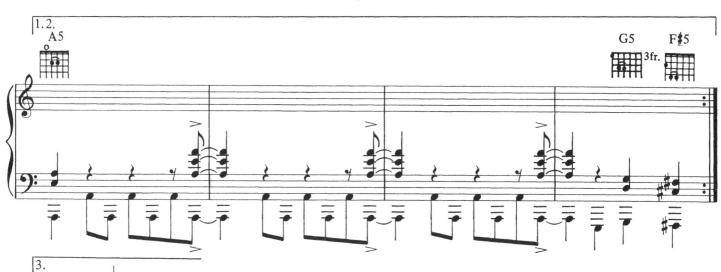

3.
Half time (♩ = 121)

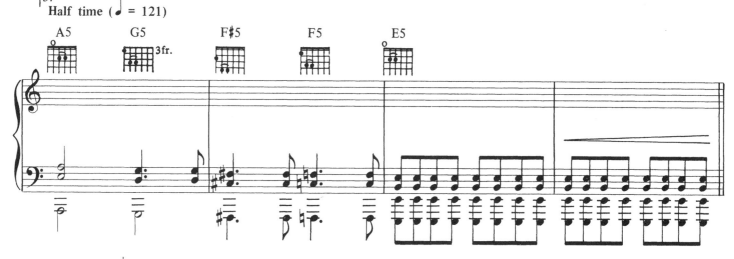

Tempo I (♩ = 242)

Play 4 times, then D.S.
(take 2nd ending) al Coda

(Guitar solo ad lib)

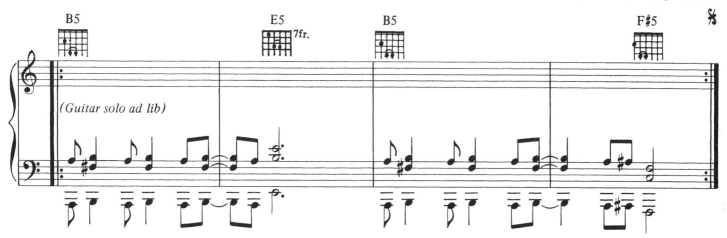

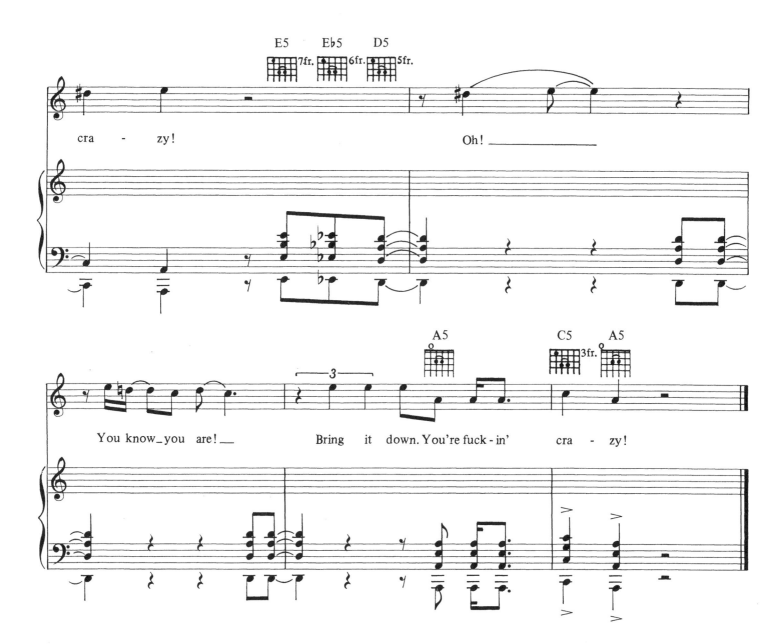

Additional Lyrics

2. Said where you goin'?
   What you gonna do?
   I been lookin' everywhere
   I been lookin' for you.
   You don't want my love, *(etc.)*

3. Say boy, where you comin' from?
   Where'd ya get that point of view?
   When I was younger
   Said I knew someone like you.
   And they said you don't want my love, *(etc.)*

Anything Goes

Words and Music by
W. Axl Rose, Slash,
Izzy Stradlin', Duff McKagan,
Steven Adler and Christopher Weber

Moderately fast ♩ = 148

1. I been think-in' 'bout, think-in' 'bout sex! Al-ways hun-gry for some-thin' that I
2. *See additional lyrics*

have-n't had yet. ___ Well may-be, ba-by, you got some-thin' to lose. ___

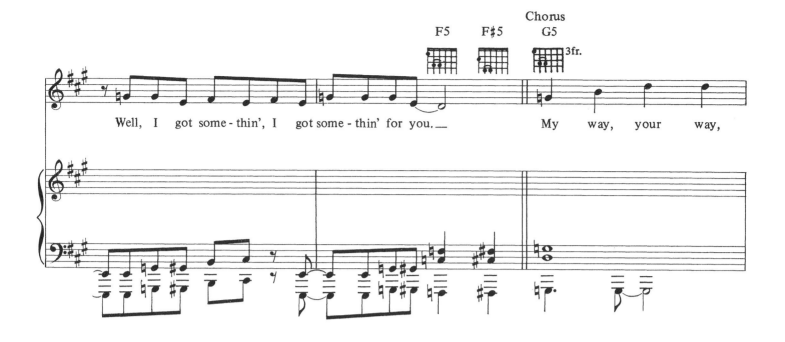

Well, I got some-thin', I got some-thin' for you.___ My way, your way,

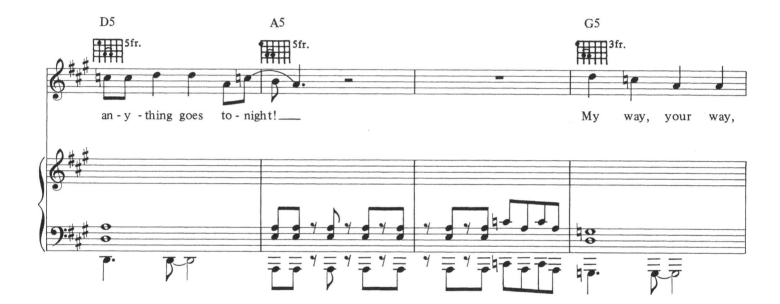

an-y-thing goes to-night!___ My way, your way,

an-y-thing goes_ to-...   an-y-thing goes to-ni-

96

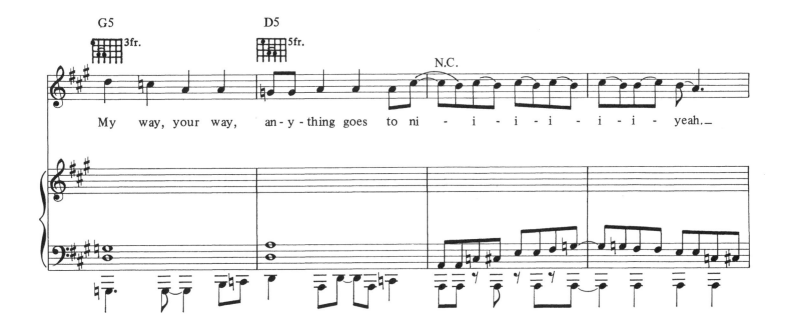

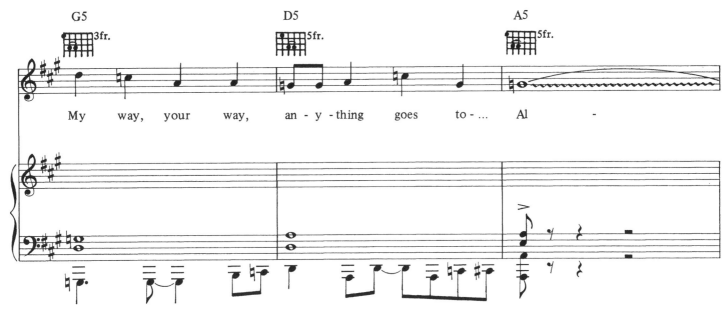

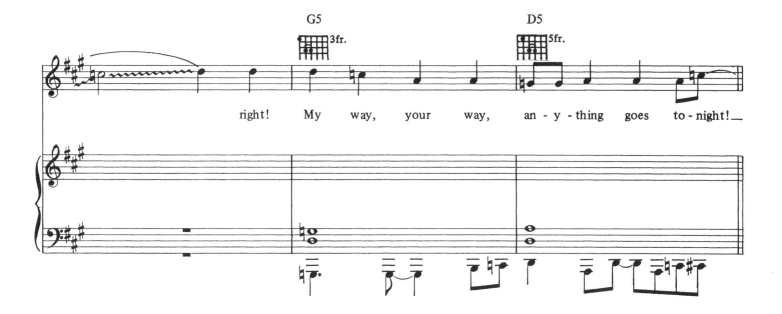

right! My way, your way, an - y - thing goes to-night!___

Slightly faster ♩ = 156; Triplet feel (♪♪ = ♩³♪)

To - night!___   To - night!___

To - night!___   An - y - thing goes to - night.___

Additional Lyrics

2. Panties 'round your knees with your ass in debris,
Doin' dat grind with a push and squeeze.
Tied up, tied down, up against the wall.
Be my rubbermade baby an' we can do it all. *(To Chorus)*

Rocket Queen

Words and Music by
W. Axl Rose, Slash,
Izzy Stradlin', Duff McKagan
and Steven Adler

Moderate Rock ♩=112 F#5

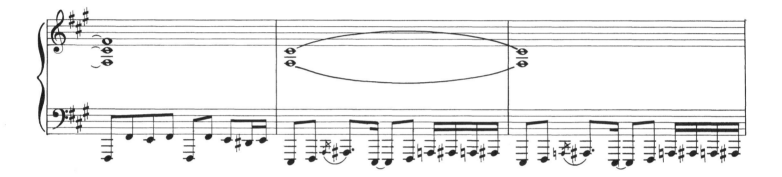

F#5

1.If I say I don't_ need an-y one,_ I can
2.I've seen ev-'ry-thing_ i-mag-'na-ble_

B5 A5   E5

say these things to you,_____ 'cause   I can turn on an-y-one_ just
pass be-fore these eyes._____ I've had   ev-'ry-thing that's tan-gi-ble,_

F#5   B5

like I turned on you. I've got a   tongue like a ra-zor,
hon-ey, you'd be sur-prised. I'm a   sex-u-al in-nu-en-do in this

R.H.

ive.___ Here I am, _____ and you're a rock-et

queen, oh yeah.___ I might be too much, but hon-ey, you're a bit ob-

scene.___

Here I am

I see you___ stand - in',

stand - in' on__ your own._____ It's such a lone -

ly place for__ you,__ for you to be._____

If you__ need a shoul - der, or if you need a friend,__

_____ I'll__ be here__ stand - in' un - til

no oh oh woh oh oh oh ___ woh oh oh oh. ___ Ba - by,

yeah!